REDUCING POLLUTION AND WASTE

Jen Green

Chicago, Illinois

© 2011 Raintree
an imprint of Capstone Global Library, LLC
Chicago, Illinois

Visit our website at www.heinemannraintree.com

Edited by Andrew Farrow and Adam Miller
Designed by Victoria Allen
Original illustrations © Capstone Global Library Ltd.
Illustrated by Tower Designs UK Limited
Picture research by Mica Brancic
Production by Camilla Crask
Originated by Capstone Global Library Ltd.
Printed and bound in China by South China Printing Company.

15 14 13 12 11
10 9 8 7 6 5 4 3 2 1

Library of Congress Cataloging-in-Publication Data
Green, Jen.
   Reducing pollution and waste / Jen Green.
      p. cm.—(The environment challenge)
   Includes bibliographical references and index.
   ISBN 978-1-4109-4299-9 (hardbound)—ISBN 978-1-4109-4306-4 (pbk.) 1. Waste minimization—Juvenile literature. 2. Pollution prevention—Juvenile literature. I. Title.
   TD793.9.G74 2012
   363.73'7—dc22   2010052711

ISBNs:
978-1-4109-4299-9 (HC)
978-1-4109-4306-4 (PB)

Acknowledgments
The author and publishers are grateful to the following for permission to reproduce copyright material: Corbis p. 13 Photolibrary/Monsoon/© Allen Russell. P. 14 © Reuters, p. 15 © Julie Dermansky, p. 16 © Roger Ressmeyer, p. 21 Reuters/© HO, p. 25 © Ryan Pyle, p. 26 © Ed Kashi, p. 31 © Paul Souders, p. 34 © Radius Images; Getty Images p. 4 Bloomberg/Arni Saeberg, p. 5 Matt Cardy, p. 6 Susan Schulman, p. 7 Science Faction/Karen Kasmauski, p. 9 Christopher Furlong, p. 17 AFP Photo/Belga/Olivier Matthys, p. 18 AFP Photo/Neil Jones, p. 23 Iconica/Nico Kai, p. 24 AFP Photo/Indranil Mukherjee, p. 27 AFP Photo, p. 28 isifa/Libor Fojtik, p. 30 Science & Society Picture Library, p. 33 Steffen Kugler, p. 35 AFP Photo/Manan Vatsyayana, p.36 Blend Images/Ariel Skelley, p. 38 Wathiq Khuzaie, p. 39 AFP Photo/Dibyangshu Sarkar, p. 40 Taxi/Steve Ryan; Reuters p. 37; Shutterstock p. 11 © Ssuaphotos.

Cover photograph of boys looking for scrap metal in Manila's largest landfill used with permission of Getty Images/ David Greedy.

We would like to thank Michael D. Mastrandrea, Ph.D. for his invaluable help in the preparation of this book.

Every effort has been made to contact copyright holders of any material reproduced in this book. Any omissions will be rectified in subsequent printings if notice is given to the publisher.

Disclaimer
All the Internet addresses (URLs) given in this book were valid at the time of going to press. However, due to the dynamic nature of the Internet, some addresses may have changed, or sites may have changed or ceased to exist since publication. While the author and publisher regret any inconvenience this may cause readers, no responsibility for any such changes can be accepted by either the author or the publisher.

Contents

Words appearing in the text in bold, **like this**, are explained in the glossary.

Polluted Earth

When the natural world is harmed by waste, or any substance that does not belong there, we call it **pollution**. Around the world, waste and pollution are building up and threatening planet Earth.

What is pollution?

Pollution damages the world around us, including the air, water, and soil. It can take the form of a gas, liquid, or solid. Fumes from a car exhaust, **sewage** (dirty water) spilling into a river, and waste rock from a mine are all forms of pollution.

Some pollution occurs naturally. For example, volcanic eruptions, dust storms, and forest fires can all **pollute**, or dirty, the environment. However, most pollution is caused by humans.

In 2010 a volcanic eruption in Iceland produced a huge cloud of ash.

Accidentally or on purpose?

Most pollution stories that hit the headlines are caused by accidents such as oil spills. However, pollution also happens through carelessness, when people do not take the proper steps to deal with waste. For example, people and companies sometimes dump waste on purpose in rivers, in oceans, and on land. Sometimes they do so out of laziness, and sometimes they do this to save money, as waste disposal can be very expensive.

People sometimes leave piles of garbage on the street or in the countryside. This looks unsightly and can cause serious pollution.

The environment challenge

Pollution of the air, water, and soil is now threatening the well-being of our planet. Part of the problem is that in **developed countries**, meaning wealthy countries such as the United States and the United Kingdom, we live wastefully, consuming resources and creating enormous amounts of waste.

This way of life is not **sustainable**—it cannot go on forever. This is because we are using up Earth's resources faster than they can be replaced. Instead, we need to live in ways that are more sustainable.

This book will explore the problems of pollution and waste, and it will ask you to take the environment challenge. Look closely at the issues and decide what you think the best solutions are—for you and for the world.

Looking for evidence

This book contains suggestions for carrying out your own research. You can use many different sources. Library books are a good source, as are newspapers and television reports. The Internet is a useful source of information, but not all websites are reliable. Try government websites and organizations with addresses ending in ".gov" or ".org." When researching facts, try to find two separate sources.

Where Do Waste and Pollution Come From?

Industry (businesses that make things), farming, and energy production are all sources of **pollution**. So are towns and cities. Every one of us produces waste as we go about our daily lives. As the number of people on Earth increases, so do levels of waste and pollution.

Industry and manufacturing

Humans have produced waste and pollution ever since we lived in caves. But serious pollution dates from the early 1800s, when people in Europe and North America began burning coal. They did so to create the energy they needed to drive machinery, but this produced smoke and **soot**. As more countries developed industries, this pollution increased.

Today, factories process natural materials, called raw materials, to produce thousands of different chemicals, metals, and plastics. Some industries produce poisonous waste.

Farming

Farming also causes pollution. Most modern farmers use chemicals called **fertilizers** to increase plant growth. Crops are sprayed with chemicals called herbicides and **pesticides** to kill weeds and insects. These chemicals harm living things in the soil and in nearby rivers. Traces of herbicides and pesticides are now found in almost all living things.

Mining causes serious pollution. This gold miner in South America is using a substance called mercury to separate gold from river gravel. Mercury poisons life in the river.

Hunger for energy

Our ever-growing energy needs are another major source of pollution. Coal, oil, and natural gas, known as **fossil fuels**, are the world's main energy source. However, burning fossil fuels produces pollution, which is affecting the environment (see pages 20–21). Supplies of fossil fuels are also limited, so their use cannot continue forever.

Nuclear energy is an alternative energy source that does not routinely produce air pollution. However, it does produce highly dangerous waste. This waste is **radioactive**, meaning it gives off tiny electronic rays, and it remains harmful for thousands of years. No one knows how to dispose of this radioactive waste safely, so it is just stored in sealed containers, usually underground. The nuclear industry claims its safety procedures are strict, but many people believe radioactive waste is a huge safety risk.

The five Ws

Over the course of your research, you will find information from different sources. It is very important to look closely at this material, judging its accuracy and reliability. You can do this by asking five basic questions, known as the "five Ws": Who? What? Where? When? Why?

For example, do research to find different perspectives on nuclear energy. You could ask yourself: Who wrote this text, and why? Would a certain organization present a certain view? Is the text offering hard evidence, or an opinion? When was it written—is it up-to-date?

Radioactive waste is monitored by nuclear industry workers who need to wear protective suits.

WORD BANK

fossil fuel	fuel that is made of decomposed plants or animals that lived long ago
industry	type of work that creates something to be sold
nuclear energy	form of energy that is made by splitting atoms of a metal called uranium
radioactive	meaning it gives off harmful rays. The waste remains dangerous for thousands of years.

Domestic waste

Household waste presents a huge problem. In the United States, each person throws away approximately 2 kilograms (4 pounds) of garbage each day. That means that a family of four throws away about 2,700 kilograms (6,000 pounds) of garbage each year.

Waste produced by cities, towns, and other settled areas is called **municipal solid waste (MSW)**. This includes garbage from stores, offices, restaurants, schools, and hospitals, as well as homes. MSW includes large amounts of food scraps and huge quantities of paper, cardboard, glass, plastic, metal, clothing, and old machinery.

Problem packaging

The contents of the average garbage can include huge amounts of packaging — the wrappings that contain the food and other goods we buy from stores and supermarkets. Some packaging is needed to protect fragile goods from damage, but a lot of it is designed to make products look more attractive, which encourages us to buy them. Almost all packaging is thrown away almost immediately. This presents a huge waste of **natural resources** (resources provided by nature), energy, and money.

This pie chart shows the proportion of different materials disposed of by a typical household in a Western country like the United States or Germany.

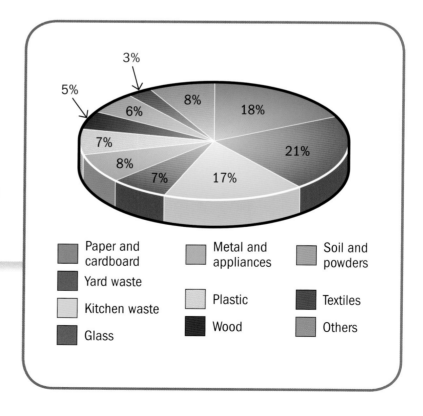

3%
5%
8%
6%
18%
7%
21%
8%
7%
17%

	Paper and cardboard		Metal and appliances		Soil and powders
Yard waste					
	Kitchen waste		Plastic		Textiles
	Glass		Wood		Others

Waste collection

In many countries, local governments arrange for garbage to be collected from homes. This valuable service gets paid for by people's taxes. Governments then spend huge amounts of money disposing of MSW safely.

"In 2008, Americans generated about 250 million tons of trash and **recycled** and **composted** (see page 40) 83 million tons of this material (approximately one-third)."

U.S. Environmental Protection Agency (EPA)

Find out more
Many local governments provide a breakdown of MSW in terms of materials such as paper, glass, metal, and plastic. Log onto your local government's website to see what you can find. You could also ask at your local library.

Some local governments collect materials for recycling at the curbside. Others provide facilities at special recycling centers.

WORD BANK

municipal solid waste (MSW)	waste produced by cities, towns, and other settled areas
natural resource	resource provided by nature
recycle	save garbage so it can be turned into another product

Will it rot?

The materials we throw away have changed a lot over the years. One hundred years ago, most waste was made up of **organic** (natural) materials such as paper, wood, wool, and cloth. These materials **biodegrade**, or rot away, quickly. In the natural world, plant and animal remains are constantly broken down by insects, worms, and bacteria. This natural recycling returns nutrients to the soil, which nourishes plants.

Today, however, garbage contains a lot of **synthetic** (human-made) materials, such as plastics, glass, and ceramics. These materials take a long time to biodegrade, and some never break down at all.

Everyday energy

Energy use is a source of pollution. This is because most of the energy we use has been created from fossil fuels, such as coal and natural gas. The burning of fossil fuels produces pollution (see pages 20 and 23). We use energy every time we switch on a light, watch television, or use a computer. Electricity is such a convenient source of energy that most of us waste it—for example, when we leave machines on "standby," rather than turning them off.

We can also cause pollution when we travel from place to place. Cars, buses, trains, and planes run on gasoline, diesel, or kerosene, which are all made from oil. As these fuels burn, they give off the waste gases carbon monoxide, sulfur dioxide, and nitrogen oxide, all of which harm living things. Traveling by car produces far more pollution per person than using buses or trains, so try to use public transportation wherever you can.

Find out more

Investigate the materials used in the packaging found in your home. Paper and corrugated cardboard, glass, aluminum, and steel are commonly used in packaging. So are plastics such as foam and polystyrene. Use the table to figure out how long each material you find will take to decompose.

Decomposition time	Name of object
2–4 weeks	Paper
1–3 months	Leaves
6 months	Fruit peel
5 years	Drink carton
10+ years	Plastic bags
50+ years	Plastic food container
80 years	Aluminum can
100 years	Tin can
400+ years	Plastic bottle
500+ years	Glass bottle
Never	Many foam plastics

The table shows the time it takes for organic and synthetic materials to rot.

Harmful waste

Some of the wastes we produce at home are also **toxic**, or poisonous. Paints, weed killers, bleach, and detergent all contain harmful chemicals that should be disposed of carefully. Your local government can advise on this. Untreated **sewage** can also cause health problems. In **developed countries**, wastewater containing sewage is usually treated, making it safe to return to rivers and streams.

Vehicles are a major cause of pollution in cities and near highways.

WORD BANK

biodegrade	rot away naturally
organic	made from natural materials
synthetic	made by humans, not nature
toxic	poisonous

The Impact of Waste and Pollution

Pollution passes through the air, water, or soil to harm the environment. In each case, the process is different. Winds help to spread air pollution. **Pollutants** (polluting substances) dissolve in water and are spread by river and ocean currents. Pollutants in the soil are spread in dust blown by wind or by water that trickles through the soil.

Chain of life

Once in the environment, pollutants harm living things. Plants, animals, and people absorb pollutants through the skin, as they breathe or take in food and water.

All forms of life are part of a **food chain**. A food chain is a collection of living things in which different life-forms eat life-forms from the level below them. Pollution affects many types of living things when it enters a food chain. Tiny organisms (living things) near the bottom of the chain commonly absorb pollutants. The pollutants then pass on to the larger creatures that prey on the smaller ones. The pollutants then build up in the predators that eat a lot of **contaminated** prey, meaning prey that have been exposed to pollution. These predators include eagles, sharks, polar bears—and humans.

Chemicals used in farming are absorbed by insects and then pass up the food chain to birds of prey such as hawks and owls.

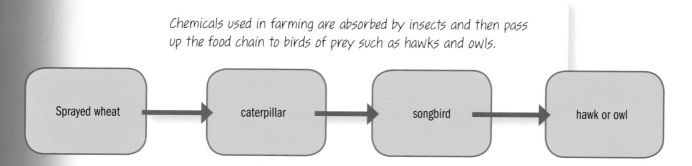

| Sprayed wheat | → | caterpillar | → | songbird | → | hawk or owl |

Air pollution

Pure, healthy air is essential to all living things. However, in many parts of the world, the air contains many pollutants. Factories, power stations, and cars are some of the main polluters. **Smog** is a form of air pollution that affects many cities worldwide. This **toxic** haze forms when waste gases from vehicles react with sunlight. The dirty air can trigger allergies, coughing, and breathing problems such as asthma. Many cities are now trying to tackle smog through measures such as reducing car use in city centers.

World's smoggiest city

Mexico City has long been ranked among the world's most **polluted** cities. The Mexican capital lies in a natural bowl surrounded by mountains, which trap air pollution. When pollution reaches critical levels, school and factory hours are changed, to avoid exposing people to the worst pollution.

Recently, the city has been making a big effort to improve air quality. Vehicles are tested every six months to make sure their exhaust gases are within safe levels. City laws require motorists to leave their cars at home one day a week and use public transportation.

When pollution levels are high in Mexico City, many people wear masks when they go outdoors.

WORD BANK

contaminate	pollute
food chain	way of describing how living things eat other living things from the level below them
pollutant	substance that harms the air, water, or land
smog	poisonous, dirty haze that forms in the air when polluting gases react with sunlight

River pollution

Plants, animals, and people depend on fresh water for survival. However, factories, farms, and cities near rivers and lakes often affect the water quality. Factories located along riverbanks often allow their waste to enter rivers, where it pollutes the area downstream.

Fertilizers from farmland or **sewage** from cities can also pollute rivers, harming fish and other water creatures. People can catch diseases such as cholera from drinking polluted water.

Tainted oceans

Most pollutants dumped in rivers end up in the ocean. For this reason, coastal waters and areas where rivers feed into oceans have high levels of pollution. People sometimes use the deep waters out at sea to dump garbage, including toxic chemicals and **radioactive** waste. Scientists have discovered that even small amounts of this toxic pollution can damage marine food chains.

Oil spills from offshore **oil rigs** and tankers can cause major environmental disasters. But routine leaks from cracked pipes and damaged tankers may also cause significant harm over time.

In January 2000, 100,000 cubic meters (3.5 million cubic feet) of deadly cyanide from a Romanian gold mine leaked into the Tisza River, in eastern Europe. It killed wildlife as far as 400 kilometers (250 miles) downriver.

The Gulf oil spill

In April 2010, a catastrophic oil spill occurred in the Gulf of Mexico, following an explosion on a deep-water oil rig 60 kilometers (41 miles) off the Louisiana coast. The oil company British Petroleum (BP) was using the rig. Following the explosion, which killed 11 workers, oil began to gush from the damaged well into the sea, covering around 70,000 square kilometers (27,000 square miles) of ocean by the end of May.

BP initially downplayed the disaster, declaring that the spill was "relatively tiny" compared to the size of the Gulf, which covers 1.5 million square kilometers (580,000 square miles). At first BP declared that the environmental impact would probably be slight. The campaign group Friends of the Earth disagreed, with a spokesperson saying, "The environmental implications of the oil spill in the Gulf are vast. . . . Marine life can be poisoned through ingesting the oil. . . . Contamination from oil can also disrupt the food chain as a whole."

By June the spill was rated the worst in U.S. history. In mid-July, BP managed to cap the well, but by then the oil had polluted hundreds of miles of coastline.

A worker sucks spilled oil from the coastal waters of the Gulf of Mexico in August 2010. The total bill for the clean-up and compensation may be as high as $20 billion.

Pollution and waste in the soil

Soil is a precious resource that is essential for plants to grow. And plants are essential to humans, as they provide our food. However, soil can be contaminated by **industry**, mining, and agriculture—and by the dumping of household waste.

In many **developing countries** (meaning poorer countries), garbage is dumped in open areas. Major cities such as Lagos, in Nigeria, and Manila, in the Philippines, are surrounded by huge heaps of rotting waste, which attract rats and flies and can cause disease.

Landfills

"Seventy percent of U.S. municipal solid waste gets buried in landfills."

Clean Air Council

In the United States, United Kingdom, and many other **developed countries**, most household waste ends up in pits called **landfills**.

Landfill sites present two main pollution risks. If the pit is not properly sealed, tainted water can leak into the surrounding soil or contaminate local water supplies. In addition, rotting garbage produces **methane** gas, which can explode if it is not drawn off safely. At many garbage sites, methane is collected and burned so that it can be used as a source of energy.

Disposing of our garbage is a major problem worldwide. Many countries are rapidly running out of space to build landfill sites.

Recycling

Environmental groups, waste experts, and local authorities say that **recycling** will play an increasingly important role in waste disposal. Recycling materials such as glass, paper, and aluminum cans saves **natural resources** such as minerals and timber, reduces energy, and cuts waste. However, recycling plants are expensive to build and operate, and not all materials are easy to recycle. (See pages 38 and 39 for more about recycling.)

What would YOU do ?

Imagine you work for a local government. Existing landfill sites in your area are full, and you need to recommend the best way forward. Would you order a study to find new landfill sites? Would you look into **incineration**? Or would you spend money on new recycling centers?

Incineration is an effective means of waste disposal. However, few people want it done near their homes, for fear of pollution.

WORD BANK
developing country   country where people do not have a high standard of living
incineration   when something is burned
landfill   large pit where garbage is packed down and covered with soil
methane   gas produced by rotting garbage

Local and Global Pollution

Some types of **pollution** affect just a local area. For example, smoke from a backyard barbecue only affects the immediate neighborhood. Other forms of pollution can travel long distances. For example, **industrial pollutants** have been found in the bodies of Arctic animals such as polar bears, which live hundreds of miles from any city or factory.

Passive smoking

Cigarette smoke is an example of harmful localized pollution. Tobacco smoke contains many dangerous substances, including carbon monoxide, nicotine, and tar, that are linked to cancer, lung infections, and heart disease. These pollutants can affect not only the smoker, but also other people in the same area. When people other than the smoker are affected, this is called passive smoking. Luckily, smoking is now banned in public places in many countries.

Transboundary pollution

Pollution in the air or water can travel huge distances, crossing national borders. This is called **transboundary pollution**. **Acid rain** is an example of transboundary pollution. Acid rain forms when nitrous oxides and sulfur dioxide from cars and factories mix with water vapor (water in gas form) in the air. The acidic moisture may drift hundreds of miles before falling as rain or snow. When acid rain is absorbed by tree roots and leaves, whole forests can die. It may also seep into lakes and rivers and then poison fish.

Cigarette smoke affects not only the smoker, as it also affects other people nearby.

The Chernobyl disaster

Nuclear reactors are places where **nuclear energy** is created. When the first nuclear reactors opened in the 1950s, the technology was hailed as a breakthrough. By the mid-1980s, hundreds of nuclear plants were providing energy in the United States, Great Britain, France, Germany, and Japan.

But in 1986, a nuclear reactor at Chernobyl, in Ukraine, caught fire and exploded. An enormous cloud of **radiation** drifted on the wind over much of Europe. When rain fell in Scandinavia and the United Kingdom, pasture and farmland were **contaminated**. Crops and the milk and meat from grazing animals had to be destroyed.

Following the Chernobyl disaster, many countries abandoned their nuclear programs. However, in the early 2000s, nuclear energy again became more attractive to governments because of new awareness of the dangers of burning **fossil fuels**.

Some 150,000 square kilometers (60,000 square miles) in Belarus, Russia, and Ukraine were contaminated by the Chernobyl disaster. People living as far as 330 kilometers (200 miles) from Chernobyl had to be evacuated from their homes. Scientists estimate that 10,000 people in the area have now died of illnesses caused by radiation.

WORD BANK
acid rain rain that is slightly acidic because of air pollution
radiation radioactive energy that can harm or kill people if they are exposed to it.
transboundary pollution pollution that crosses borders between countries

Global warming

Air pollution on a global scale is thought to be affecting Earth's weather patterns. Certain gases occur naturally in Earth's **atmosphere**, the envelope of gases that surrounds Earth. These gases, including **carbon dioxide** and **methane**, act like the glass in a greenhouse. They trap some of the heat that reaches Earth from the Sun, preventing it from escaping into space. This is called the greenhouse effect, and the gases behind it are called **greenhouse gases**.

More greenhouse gases

The natural greenhouse effect helps to produce temperatures that suit living things on Earth. However, over the course of the last 200 years, we have been adding increasing amounts of carbon dioxide to the atmosphere. This is because as factories, power stations, and vehicles burn fossil fuels, they release carbon dioxide. Carbon dioxide is also released when we clear forested land. Meanwhile, farming practices such as growing rice and rearing cattle are adding methane to the atmosphere.

Scientists are now convinced that increased levels of these greenhouse gases are causing Earth to heat up—an effect called **global warming**. A few people believe global warming is part of a natural cycle of warming and cooling, but nearly all scientists are convinced that air pollution is to blame for the temperature rise.

Feeling the heat

Since 1900 global temperatures have risen by 0.6 °C (1 °F). In polar regions they have risen faster, by up to 2 to 3 °C (3.6 to 5.4 °F). The polar ice has started to melt, swelling the volume of water in the oceans. In the 1900s, this helped to cause sea levels to rise by 20 to 30 centimeters (8 to 12 inches).

If world levels of greenhouse gases continue to rise, global warming could accelerate. World temperatures could rise by 2 to 3.5 °C (3.6 to 6.3 °F) by 2100. If this happens, rising sea levels could threaten low-lying countries and islands worldwide. Much of Egypt, Bangladesh, and whole island nations such as the Maldives could disappear.

Make a KWL chart

Find out more about global warming using library books, news reports, and the Internet. A "KWL chart" will help you organize your research. "K" stands for "What I **k**now"; "W" stands for "What I **w**ant to know"; and "L" stands for "What I **l**earned."

Use the information you have learned in this book to fill in the first column. Questions go in column 2, and new facts from your research go in column 3.

What I Know	What I want to know	What I learned
Scientists believe temperatures on Earth are increasing.	What are the likely effects of global warming?	

This diagram shows the greenhouse effect.

3. Most radiation is absorbed by Earth and warms it.

2. Some radiation is reflected by Earth and its atmosphere.

4. The warm Earth emits lower energy infrared radiation. Some is absorbed by greenhouse gas molecules. Less heat escapes and so Earth's temperature rises.

1. High energy radiation from the Sun passes through the atmosphere.

CASE STUDY

Threatened islands

The Maldives are a group of small coral islands in the Indian Ocean. No part of the Maldives is more than 2.3 meters (7.5 feet) above sea level. A 1-meter (3.3-foot) sea level rise would put 80 percent of the islands underwater. If global warming continues, the whole nation could be lost to the sea by 2100.

In 2009 the government of the Maldives staged a cabinet meeting underwater in scuba gear. It did this to publicize the dangers the islands are facing.

WORD BANK
atmosphere   envelope of gases that surrounds Earth
carbon dioxide colorless gas we breathe out, made of oxygen and carbon
global warming rising temperatures worldwide, caused by increasing levels of greenhouse gases

Who Produces Pollution and Waste?

Everybody produces some waste and **pollution**. However, not all nations contribute equally to these problems. People in **developed countries** produce far more waste and pollution than people in **developing countries**.

Throwaway society

In wealthy countries such as the United States, people have a comfortable lifestyle. Our homes are full of machines such as vacuum cleaners and dishwashers, which save us from doing extra work. Most families have at least one car, computer, and television. Many of us buy a new computer and cell phone every few years, and when machines break down we often buy a new one rather than repairing the old one. We spend money on the latest fashions and throw away clothes we feel are out of style. We also waste a lot of food that we do not eat.

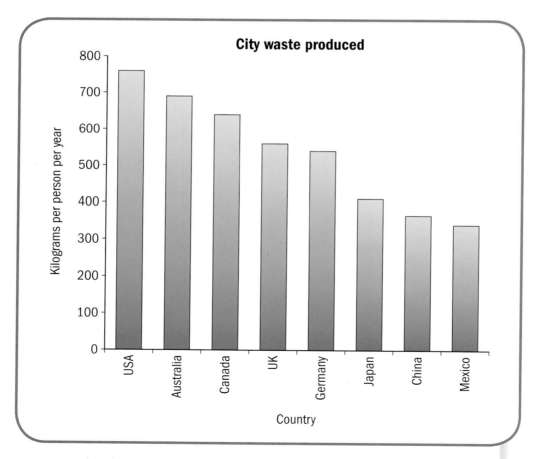

This chart compares the volume of **municipal solid waste** produced per person in selected countries for the year 2000.

Amazingly, most of the things we buy are thrown away within just six months. Of course, this creates a huge waste disposal problem. Moreover, a high percentage of the garbage we throw away is made up of materials such as plastic and metal, which take hundreds of years to **biodegrade**.

High energy use

In addition to creating waste, the technology we use in developed countries uses huge amounts of energy. Experts say that people living in wealthy nations, representing just 25 percent of the world's **population** (people), use 70 percent of all the energy used worldwide. Since most of this energy is created by burning **fossil fuels**, people in developed countries produce far more **carbon dioxide** per person than those in developing countries. So, we are more responsible for **global warming**. On the bright side, wealthier nations have the money to invest in new technologies that reduce pollution (see page 33).

(see page 33)

Litter survey

Carry out a survey of litter in a public place such as a shopping center. Notice the amount of litter that comes from fast food packaging, such as cardboard cartons and soda cups or cans. Write a report and send it to your local government, suggesting what could be done to reduce litter. For example, should garbage cans be emptied more regularly? If so, would taxpayers be happy to pay for this?

In developed countries, many people regularly eat "fast foods" such as hamburgers and French fries. Fast foods come wrapped in a lot of packaging.

Waste not, want not

In regions such as Africa, parts of Asia, and South America, people have far less money to spend on possessions. Relatively few people have televisions, cars, and computers. Many areas, particularly in the countryside, lack electricity grids, and millions of people live in poverty.

Because there is less money to waste, vehicles and all kinds of equipment are carefully repaired rather than being thrown away. All this means that people in developing countries use less energy and generate a lot less waste. In addition, a much higher percentage of waste is **organic** and quickly rots away.

Developing industries

Nonetheless, in the last 20 years, life has changed in many developing countries, as nations such as China, India, and Brazil have modernized quickly. Such nations have a rapidly growing middle class, which wants cars, televisions, computers, and other trappings of a Western lifestyle. Many people believe that when a country becomes **industrialized** (develops its **industries**) and opens factories and power plants, this provides the key to higher living standards and the solution to poverty.

In China, India, and other developing countries, new factories, mines, and power stations open regularly. Every week there are more cars on the roads. Populations in these countries are also quickly rising. All this means that energy use is rising—as are waste and pollution levels. However, some developing countries have little money to spend on technology that can reduce pollution. As a result, many cities and **industrial** areas in the developing world are heavily **polluted**.

Mass movement to cities such as Mumbai in India causes overcrowding. Rapidly expanding slums lack the facilities to deal with **sewage** and waste.

China, an emerging giant

China has industrialized very rapidly since the 1990s. As its industries have developed, its energy needs have also grown by leaps and bounds—and pollution levels have risen, too. Cities such as Beijing suffer from very high levels of air pollution, which has been linked to thousands of deaths a year. In 2006 China overtook the United States as the world's number-one producer of carbon dioxide. China says Western nations are quick to blame it for the world's pollution, but happy to buy cheap, mass-produced Chinese goods. The production of these goods in factories is a big cause of pollution.

In 2007—2008, China opened an average of one new power plant per week.

WORD BANK

industrialize when a country develops its industries, so that many factories and power plants open

Not in my backyard

Countries are not always responsible for waste and pollution within their borders. **Multinational** companies (companies that operate in several countries) set up mines, factories, and **oil rigs** abroad to take advantage of **natural resources** or cheap labor costs there. These companies often benefit from loose pollution laws and lower safety standards in other countries. They are often accused of being less careful about pollution abroad than they would on their own soil.

CASE STUDY

Oil in the Niger Delta

The Niger Delta in Nigeria, West Africa, is one of the world's largest wetlands. Home to over 30 million people, it also has very rich supplies of oil. Oil has been extracted (removed) here since the 1960s by Nigeria and also by Shell, a multinational oil company.

Oil has generated an estimated $600 billion in the last 50 years, but it has led to widespread pollution through oil spills, leaks, and the dumping of waste. The human rights group Amnesty International reports: "Many people in the oil-producing areas have to drink, cook with and wash in polluted water, and eat fish **contaminated** with oil and other toxins [poisons]." In contrast to the huge profits made by the oil companies, most local people live in poverty, and unemployment and violence are widespread problems.

Soil in the farmland surrounding the Niger Delta is heavily polluted, which makes it difficult to grow food.

The Bhopal disaster

In the 1980s, the U.S. chemical company Union Carbide operated a **pesticides** factory near the city of Bhopal, in India. In December 1984, a major leak of **toxic** gases killed more than 7,000 people. Over 15,000 have since died as a result of the contamination. The incident was one of the world's worst industrial disasters. Union Carbide, now called Dow Chemical, has never properly cleaned the area. Local soil and water sources are still polluted.

For 25 years, campaigners tried to bring the company to justice. In June 2010, seven local managers were found guilty of causing "death by negligence" and given a sentence of two years in prison. But the U.S. boss of the company escaped trial. A local campaigner commented on the verdict: "Such low sentences show how we bow down before multinational companies."

Many people lost their sight after the poison gas leak in Bhopal.

What would YOU do ?

Should countries pay for all the pollution that happens within their borders? Or should multinational companies that pollute the area pay for the cleanup? If so, how could you make sure this happens?

Tackling Pollution

Pollution can be tackled in two main ways. One is to clean up the damage done. The other is to remove or reduce the source of pollution. It is almost always far cheaper, as well as better for the environment, to follow this approach and reduce pollution at the source.

"Polluter pays"

The "polluter pays" is a principle that is applied to environmental cleanup work wherever possible. This means that the company responsible for the pollution is required to fund the cleanup effort. However, it is not always easy to get companies to accept responsibility, especially in cases of **transboundary pollution**.

Cleaning up oil spills

When a major oil spill occurs at sea, the cleanup effort can cost millions, and even billions, of dollars. Floating barriers called booms are often used to contain the oil. The oil may then be skimmed off the surface. If oil washes ashore, high-pressure hoses may be used to disperse it, while pumps are used to vacuum it up. Birds, seals, and other animals clogged with oil must be washed individually, but most die anyway. In the long run, it is far cheaper for companies to tighten their own pollution controls in the first place, rather than be responsible for such a massive cleanup effort.

Make a problem-solving model

A diagram called a problem-solving model is a way to organize facts about complex issues. The problem box states the problem. Possible solutions and their effects are set out in boxes below. The conclusion box shows what you decide is the best option. Copy and fill in this diagram to summarize the facts about tackling acid rain.

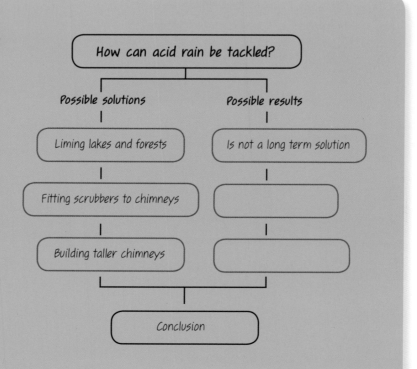

How can acid rain be tackled?

Possible solutions

Possible results

Liming lakes and forests

Is not a long term solution

Fitting scrubbers to chimneys

Building taller chimneys

Conclusion

Tackling acid rain

The lakes and forests of Japan are **polluted** by **acid rain**. This is caused by the spread of pollution from factories and power plants in China.

Scientists are trying to come up with ways to address the problem. Factory chimneys can be made taller, which reduces local pollution—but it does not prevent it from spreading in the wind. Acidic lakes can be treated by dumping a substance called lime on them. Lime counters the effect of the acid. However, this process is expensive, and its effects are not permanent.

A better solution is to reduce pollution at the source. Japan is paying for filters called scrubbers to be fitted to power plants and factories in China, in the hope that it will reduce acid rain damage back home.

A plane dumps lime onto the Sous Dam in the Czech Republic.

29

Anti-pollution laws

Worldwide efforts to reduce pollution took off in the 1970s, thanks in part to the work of environmental groups such as Greenpeace and Friends of the Earth, which helped to raise public awareness about environmental problems. The United States, United Kingdom, and many other countries passed laws to clean up the air, water, and soil. In many countries, government groups were set up to monitor pollution and make sure businesses obeyed the rules.

Find out more

Find out more about the work of environmental protection agencies by visiting your government's website. Type "environmental protection" and the name of your country into a search engine.

Cleaning up cars

The United States, Japan, and most **developed countries** have passed laws to reduce the pollution released by vehicles. In the early 1900s, lead was added to gasoline to improve engine efficiency. Later, scientists discovered that lead pollution could cause brain damage. As a result, lead-free gasoline was introduced. In the United States, this measure reduced lead levels by over 90 percent.

In the United States, Great Britain, and most European countries, devices called catalytic converters are fitted to car exhausts to filter out harmful waste gases, or **emissions**. In many U.S. states, Great Britain, western Europe, Japan, and Australia, car emissions are tested regularly, and vehicles that fail the test are not allowed on the road.

The dark blue area on this satellite image shows where the ozone level is lowest. Ozone loss over Antarctica has raised ultraviolet levels in Australia, increasing the number of cases of skin cancer there.

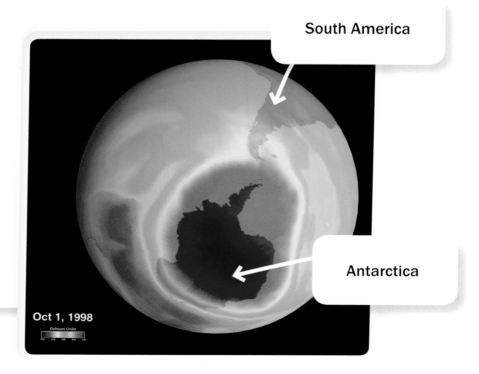

South America

Antarctica

Oct 1, 1998

Dobson Units

International agreements

International agreements can help to reduce forms of transboundary pollution such as acid rain. Individual nations decide whether to sign these agreements. In 1987 countries around the world came together to tackle the problem of ozone loss. The **ozone layer** is a layer of gas high in the **atmosphere**. It filters out the harmful **radiation** in sunlight, called ultraviolet rays, that can trigger skin cancer in humans.

In 1985 scientists discovered that the ozone layer had become much thinner, particularly over polar regions. The damage was traced to chemicals called chlorofluorocarbons (CFCs), which were used as coolants in refrigerators and to make aerosol sprays such as hairspray. In 1987 most nations signed a landmark agreement called the Montreal Protocol, which outlawed the use of CFCs. Scientists believe that this measure should help to restore the ozone layer by about 2050.

An international agreement called the Law of the Sea Treaty has helped to reduce pollution in the oceans.

WORD BANK
emission   release of a gas
ozone layer   layer of gas found in the atmosphere that prevents harmful ultraviolet
              rays in sunlight from reaching Earth

31

Tackling climate change

Solving ozone loss is relatively easy compared to tackling **climate change**, which is the change in the temperature, rainfall, or wind of a region. These changes are brought about by **global warming**. Many scientists believe that climate change is the most serious environmental problem of our time.

The most obvious way to tackle the problem is to reduce emissions of **greenhouse gases** like **carbon dioxide**. This can be achieved by burning fewer **fossil fuels**. However, this is easier said than done.

Since the 1990s, the world's nations have met at climate conferences to try to agree to cuts in greenhouse gases. In 1997 many nations signed the Kyoto Protocol, pledging to reduce their emissions by 5 percent by 2012. However, the United States did not sign, because it believed the agreement would harm the country's economy. The 2009 climate conference in Copenhagen failed to reach agreement on further cuts.

What would YOU do ?

How do you think the problem of climate change should best be tackled? Make a problem-solving model like the one on page 28 to organize your ideas. One solution would be to only use clean energy sources. For this to work, however, we would all need to drastically reduce our energy use.

This chart shows the world's 10 leading carbon dioxide producers in 2006. (Note: Although each U.S. citizen produces far more carbon dioxide than each person in China, China produces more carbon dioxide overall because it has a much larger **population**.)

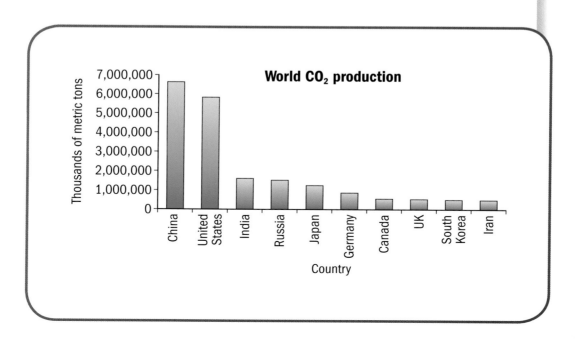

World CO$_2$ production

Is technology the answer?

Many technical solutions to the problem of global warming have been put forward. One is to bury carbon dioxide on the bed of the oceans. Another idea is to position giant mirrors in space to reflect sunlight. Some ideas are unrealistic. Others are very expensive. But environmentalists and scientists all over the world believe we should work toward reducing greenhouse gas emissions, rather than relying entirely on technology.

Alternative energies

Since burning fossil fuels is the main cause of climate change, alternative energy sources are the best way forward. **Nuclear energy** is one option, but, as we have seen, it produces very harmful waste.

Energy sources such as wind power, **solar** (Sun) power, and hydroelectric (water) power are part of the answer. These technologies cause very little pollution. Moreover, they are **renewable**, meaning they will never run out. Hydrogen fuel cells are another future energy source. Fuel cells are machines that make energy using gases such as hydrogen. But these sources alone do not provide enough energy.

All of these sources have drawbacks, so we will probably need to rely on several. Beyond finding new energy sources, though, we simply need to use less energy.

World leaders discuss global warming at the 2009 climate conference in Copenhagen.

Saving energy

Our everyday use of energy at home, at school, and at work creates more greenhouse gases and pollution. On the bright side, this means that each and every one of us can help to cut pollution. We can do this by using less energy, as well as using cleaner fuels.

There are literally hundreds of ways to save energy. Here are a few easy ones:

- Switch off lights when you leave the room.
- Use low-energy light bulbs, which use one-fifth of the energy of ordinary bulbs.
- Switch off and unplug machines such as computers and televisions, rather than leaving them in "standby" mode.
- Save energy used for heating by making sure your home is well insulated, meaning it is lined with materials that prevent heat from escaping. Fix drafty doors and windows and turn the central heating down a little. In the United States and in many other countries, tax breaks are available to help people make homes more energy-efficient.

Tackling transportation

Transportation produces about 30 percent of all greenhouse gas emissions. The average family car produces more than 4 tonnes (4.4 tons) of carbon dioxide a year. Can you try to reduce car use by walking, cycling, using the school bus, or using public transportation to get to school? The U.S. government and other governments have provided tax breaks when people buy fuel-efficient cars. Can you persuade your family to switch to a fuel-efficient model? You can also ask drivers to slow down a little, which will use less fuel.

Always switch your computer off after you have finished using it!

New fuels for cars

Car manufacturers are now developing vehicles that run on fuels that cause less pollution. The Toyota Prius is a hybrid car, which mean that it runs on both gasoline and electricity. However, electric cars still have to be recharged from electricity grids, which are mostly generated from fossil fuels. Solar- and hydrogen-fueled cars are also being developed. In North America and South America, many cars run on ethanol, a type of fuel called a biofuel that is made from crops such as sugar cane. However, growing enough biofuels to meet vehicle needs would involve converting farmland that is needed to grow food.

In recent years, many cities around the world have introduced cleaner forms of public transportation. The city of New Delhi, India, has commissioned the world's largest fleet of low-polluting buses.

Reduce, Reuse, and Recycle

Environmentalists believe that the problems of waste and **pollution** can be reduced by following the "three Rs" of waste disposal: Reduce, Reuse, and **Recycle**. The best solution of all is to reduce the amount of waste we produce in the first place. Reusing materials whenever possible is good for the environment. Recycling helps to solve the problem of waste disposal. It can also reduce pollution and litter. But environmentalists see recycling as a last resort, when neither reducing nor reusing waste is possible.

Reducing waste

We can all help to reduce the volume of waste by avoiding goods with a lot of packaging. You can ask your mail carrier not to deliver junk mail like catalogs to your home. In the United States, 100 million trees are used to produce junk mail each year.

Don't use disposable items such as plastic cutlery and paper plates. Use ordinary plates and cutlery and wash them. If you buy a "fast food" meal, ask the restaurant if it can supply the least amount of packaging possible.

Reusing materials

All sorts of materials can be reused with a little thought. Plastic tubs are very useful as containers. Glass jars can be used as pencil holders, while empty bottles can double as vases or candle-holders. Use both sides of paper before you throw it away. Magazines can be cut up to make cards. Plastic bags commonly end up as litter, but you can also reuse them in stores and supermarkets.

Try to bring a cloth bag with you to the store, so that you do not need to use plastic bags.

Litter-free city

The city of Singapore, in Southeast Asia, is virtually free of litter. This is because the authorities impose severe penalties on people who drop litter. Anyone who drops so much as a paper clip can be required to do 10 hours of community service. The maximum penalty for a first litter offense is $10,000 or a year in prison—or both. For a second offense, it is $20,000 or two years in prison. Most chewing gum is banned because of the mess used gum can make.

Singapore's government puts more limits on individual freedom than some Western democracies, in order to improve living conditions for all. Do you think other governments should follow suit? Think about the problems your own local government faces when it comes to litter and pollution. How would you feel if it followed Singapore's example?

Dropping litter is a serious offense in Singapore (see Case Study above). The man wearing a cap is being booked for dropping a cigarette butt on the street and will have to pay a fine.

Economics of recycling

A wide range of materials, including glass, aluminum, steel, paper, and plastic, can now be recycled. However, recycling is not always cost-effective. The material being recycled has to be reasonably valuable to make it worth the cost of collecting, transporting, cleaning, and reprocessing it, all of which use energy. And the recycler has to find a buyer for the recycled material in order to make money.

Is it cost-effective?

Aluminum and glass are among the materials mostly commonly recycled. Aluminum, used to make drink cans, comes from a substance called bauxite, which is heated at high temperature in a furnace. This process is expensive and uses a lot of energy. Recycling aluminum saves 95 percent of the energy used to make cans from fresh metal. Recycling glass is also cost-effective, and it saves 40 percent of the energy used to make fresh glass. Both glass and aluminium can be recycled any number of times without loss of quality.

Paper and plastic are more difficult to recycle. Paper is not very valuable, so it is more difficult to make recycling cost-effective. There are many types of plastic, and relatively few kinds can be economically recycled. Only five percent of plastic waste is recycled.

Glass for recycling is crushed and melted in a furnace.

Waste picking in Asia

In many developing countries, where money is scarce, a wide range of materials is valuable enough to recycle. Hundreds of thousands of people, including many children, make a living sorting through garbage to find materials that can be sold or reused.

In Bangalore, India, people called waste pickers sort through garbage to find materials that can be reused or resold. They process around 300 tonnes (331 tons) of waste a day, leaving just 37 tonnes (41 tons) to be dealt with by local government workers. However, this work is dirty, smelly, and can be dangerous. How would you like to spend your day sifting through piles of stinking, rotting waste?

In the Philippines, in Southeast Asia, around 60,000 people make a living sifting through waste in dumps outside Manila, the capital city. In 2000, 300 waste pickers died after heavy rain caused a heap of garbage to collapse, burying workers' makeshift homes.

Waste pickers sort though waste in a **landfill** site near Bangalore in India.

Toward zero waste

The "three Rs"—reduce, reuse, recycle—provide the key to tackling waste and litter. They are also an important part of **sustainable** living. Some environmentalists believe we should work toward eliminating waste entirely. This is called zero waste.

What would YOU do ?

Investigate the contents of your garbage can. How much of it could be reused, recycled, or composted?

A few years ago, only a small range of materials could be recycled in countries like the United States. Recycling centers only accepted glass, metal, paper, and textiles. Many people did not recycle because it took a bit more effort than simply throwing things in the trash. Today, however, the range of recyclable materials is much larger, and curbside recycling is more common. Plastics, steel, rubber, old batteries, computers, and cell phones can all be recycled. Attitudes have changed, and many people now recycle.

Buying second-hand clothes is a great way to save money, help the environment—and stay chic!

Sustainable living

Organic materials such as fruit and vegetable peelings can be turned into **compost** (rotting natural material that gardeners use to enrich the soil). Make your own compost heap or contact your local government to find out about shared compost facilities.

You could also try to do a "clear-out" at home. Clothes, toys, and books you do not want can go to a charity store. Many charity stores also take cell phones, cookware, CDs, furniture, and furnishings. Or you may be able to sell your items at a garage sale. According to the environmental group Friends of the Earth, "Most of the things we throw away could be a valuable resource for someone, somewhere." The real waste is when we throw useful materials away.

Reducing, reusing, and recycling waste help the environment in many ways. They preserve energy and precious materials and save on space for landfill. The "three Rs" and saving energy can really help to keep Earth a safe and beautiful place.

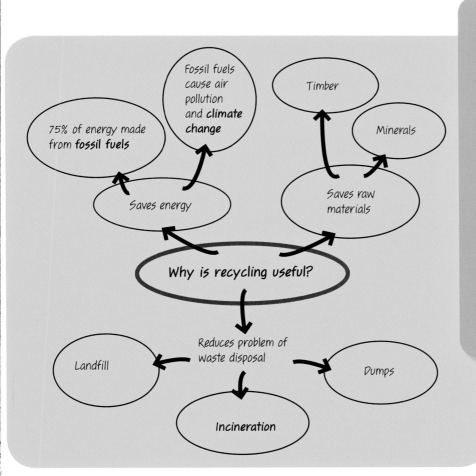

Make a concept web

A concept web can help you organize your ideas and research. Put your main research question in a box near the center. Arrange facts under subheadings linked by arrows to the main question. Look at the concept web shown here, which explores the question: "Why is recycling useful?" Now try making a concept web that tackles one aspect of pollution, such as water or car pollution. Use facts from this book and your own research.

Facts and Figures

World's worst oil spills

1977   The blowout of a well in the Norwegian Ekofisk oil field causes 307 million liters (81 million gallons) of oil to leak into the North Sea.

1978   The wrecked tanker *Amoco Cadiz* spills 258 million liters (68 million gallons) of oil into French waters, **polluting** the Brittany coast.

1979   The oil well Ixtoc 1 blows out in the Gulf of Mexico, spilling some 530 million liters (140 million gallons) of crude oil (oil in its thick, raw state).

1980   A floating oil platform collapses off Norway in the North Sea, killing 123 oil workers.

1983   The Nowruz Field platform in the Persian Gulf spills 303 million liters (80 million gallons) of oil.

1983   The Spanish tanker *Castillo de Bellver* catches fire, spilling 295 million liters (78 million gallons) of oil off the South African coast.

1988   After an explosion on the Piper Alpha **oil rig** in the North Sea, 166 workers die.

1989   The tanker *Exxon Valdez* hits a reef off the Alaskan coast, spilling more than 38 million liters (10 million gallons) of oil.

1991   During the Persian Gulf War (1990–91), Iraqi troops deliberately release 908 million to 1.3 billion liters (240 to 336 million gallons) of crude oil into the Persian Gulf from tankers off Kuwait.

1992   An oil well in Uzbekistan, in Central Asia, spills 333 million liters (88 million gallons) of oil.

2002   The damaged oil tanker *Prestige* sinks off the coast of Spain with 76 million liters (20 million gallons) of oil on board.

2005   Over 26.5 million liters (7 million gallons) of oil spill in New Orleans, Louisiana, during Hurricane Katrina from pipelines, storage tanks, and factories.

2010   The Deepwater Horizon oil rig sinks in the Gulf of Mexico following an explosion that kills 11 people. From April through June, as much as 60,000 barrels (9.5 million liters, or 2.5 million gallons) of oil per day leak into the Gulf, threatening wildlife along the Louisiana coast.

Source: www.infoplease.com/ipa/A0001451.html

World's top-five most polluted places

1. In Linfen, China, the air and water are polluted by waste gases and **pollutants** from **industry**. Cleanup status: unknown.

2. The soil in Haina, Dominican Republic, in the Caribbean, is heavily polluted by lead from battery **recycling**. No cleanup is planned.

3. In Ranipet, India, the water and soil are polluted by chemicals from the tanning (leather-making) industry. Cleanup is planned, but has not started yet.

4. In Mailuu-Suu, Kyrgyzstan, in Central Asia, the soil is **contaminated** by **radioactive** waste from a **nuclear energy** plant. Cleanup is planned with funding from the World Bank.

5. In Dzerzhinsk, Russia, the water and soil are polluted by chemicals from weapons testing. Cleanup is only in the planning stage.

Find out about the next-most polluted places by logging onto www.blacksmithinstitute.org/top10/10worst2.pdf.

Source: www.blacksmithinstitute.org/top10/10worst2.pdf

Friends of the Earth's top tips for reducing waste

- Use your curbside recycling program, if you have one.

- Avoid disposable batteries. Use rechargeable ones with **solar**-powered rechargers instead.

- Refuse plastic bags at the store. Carry a reusable bag instead.

- Buy loose fruits and vegetables from a local market or grocer rather than highly packaged goods from supermarkets.

- Try **composting** your yard and kitchen waste. Many local governments now offer advice.

- Only print things out from your computer when you really need to. If you do print, use both sides of the paper.

World's smoggiest cities

1. Mexico City, Mexico
2. São Paulo, Brazil
3. Cairo, Egypt
4. New Delhi, India
5. Shanghai, China

Source: www.timeforkids. com/TFK/kids/ns/

Glossary

acid rain rain that is slightly acidic because of air pollution

atmosphere envelope of gases that surrounds Earth

biodegrade rot away naturally

carbon dioxide colorless gas we breathe out, made of oxygen and carbon

climate change change in the regular weather patterns of a region

compost rotting natural materials that can be used to help gardens grow

contaminate pollute

developed country wealthy country where people have a high standard of living

developing country country where people do not have a high standard of living

emission release of a gas

fertilizer chemical that farmers use to make plants grow better

food chain way of describing how living things eat other living things from the level below them

fossil fuel fuel that is made of decomposed plants or animals that lived long ago. Fossil fuels include coal, oil, and natural gas.

global warming rising temperatures worldwide, caused by increasing levels of greenhouse gases

greenhouse gas gas in the atmosphere that traps the Sun's heat

incineration when something is burned

industrial relating to industry, a type of work that creates something to be sold, often through the use of factories and power plants

industrialize when a country develops its industries, so that many factories and power plants open

industry type of work that creates something to be sold, often through the use of factories and power plants

landfill large pit where garbage is packed down and covered with soil

methane gas produced by rotting garbage

multinational operating in several countries

municipal solid waste (MSW) waste produced by cities, towns, and other settled areas

natural resource resource provided by nature

nuclear energy form of energy that is made by splitting atoms of a metal called uranium

oil rig special equipment used for drilling an oil well

organic made from natural materials

ozone layer layer of gas found in the atmosphere that prevents harmful ultraviolet rays in sunlight from reaching Earth

pesticide chemical put on plants to kill plant-eating pests

pollutant substance that harms the air, water, or land

pollute when harmful substances dirty the air, water, or soil

pollution when the natural world is harmed by waste or by any substance that does not belong there

population number of people in an area

radioactive meaning it gives off harmful rays. The waste remains dangerous for thousands of years

radiation radioactive energy that can harm or kill people if they are exposed to it.

recycle save garbage so it can be turned into a new product

renewable fuel or material that can be grown or made again

sewage dirty water from homes that contains chemicals and human waste

smog poisonous, dirty haze that forms in the air when polluting gases react with sunlight

solar relating to the Sun

soot black, powdery substance, often resulting from burning fossil fuels, such as coal

sustainable when resources are managed so that they will not run out in the future, causing little damage to the environment

synthetic made by humans, not nature

toxic poisonous

transboundary pollution pollution that crosses borders between countries

Find Out More

Books

Claybourne, Anna. *Forms of Energy (Sci-Hi: Physical Science)*. Chicago: Raintree, 2010.

Faust, Daniel R. *Sinister Sludge: Oil Spills and the Environment (Jr. Graphic Environmental Dangers)*. New York: PowerKids Press, 2009.

Gorman, Jacqueline Laks. *Fossil Fuels (What If We Do Nothing?)*. Pleasantville, N.Y.: Gareth Stevens Publishing, 2009.

Green, Jen. *Reducing Air Pollution (Improving Our Environment)*. Milwaukee: Gareth Stevens Publishing, 2005.

Simon, Seymour. *Global Warming*. New York: Collins, 2010.

Solway, Andrew. *Environmental Technology (New Technology)*. Mankato, Minn.: Smart Apple Media, 2009.

Woodward, John. *Climate Change (Eyewitness)*. New York: DK Publishing, 2008.

Websites

http://kids.niehs.nih.gov/recycle.htm
This website of the National Institute of Environmental Health Sciences offers advice about how young people can reduce, reuse, and recycle.

www.epa.gov/kids/garbage.htm
This website of the U.S. Environmental Protection Agency provides lots of information about garbage and recycling.

www.epa.gov/kids/air.htm
This website of the U.S. Environmental Protection Agency provides facts about air pollution, including links that discuss climate change.

www.eere.energy.gov/kids/
This website, created by the U.S. Department of Energy, offers games, tips, and facts to help young people save energy.

www.greenpeace.org/usa/
Learn more about what the environmental group Greenpeace is doing to protect the environment.

www.foe.org
Learn more about how the environmental group Friends of the Earth is trying to save the environment.

Index